Create Rebellion

Create Rebellion

Robbie Tripp

ISBN: 9781630729004

Izzard Ink Publishing Izzard Ink, LLC
PO Box 522251
Salt Lake City, UT 84152
(415) 889-6100

Second Edition: June 2016

1 10 9 8 7 6 5 4 3 2

For information contact
Robbie Tripp www.robbietripp.com
Book and cover design by Kyson Dana

*For those who dream while awake and create
instead of sleep.*

Introduction

My phone alarm hums in the wee hours of the morning. I reach over to the nightstand and put on my glasses while trying to slowly and evenly distribute my weight so as not to wake the angelic being still sleeping next to me. I tip toe out of bed and close the bedroom door softly before making my way down the hall. The gray light of dawn is seeping through the cracks of my office window. Before I sit, I pull the window shade down a little further so the room becomes even more muted. I never touch the light switch in this room; I like to write in the dark. I plug in my space heater and place it directly next to my chair. I use it for the calming purr it makes as much as I do the warmth it provides. I open my laptop and immediately begin to type. Whatever words swirl about in my head I snatch instantly and formulate them into unstructured order. I turn subconscious into sentence, and imagination into indentation. I continue this process of unrelenting keyboard pounding for as long as inspiration will abide with me. I say things that I want to say, maybe in a way that most people might not say them. That is how I create rebellion.

I wrote this book because I believe a creative life is the most fulfilling life. I've also found that it is one of much adventure and surprise. While it's always been my goal to write books, I certainly couldn't have predicted this would be my first. I think that's typical of inspiration, and precisely what makes it so beautiful. You can't control it or plan for it, you just have to let it take you for a ride. As I sat down at my computer each morning and found this abstract yet meaningful stream of consciousness pouring out of me, I felt a difference from my usual writing sessions. While I had always imagined that my first book would be a novel or other fictional work of some kind, what came out instead is this little creative treatise, an allegorical manifesto. The words in this book found me as much as I searched for them, and I hope the inspiration from which they were born finds you as well.

As any artist will tell you, there is as much wonder and satisfaction to be found in creative pursuits as there is frustration and self-loathing. Surely there are easier ways to live than feeling a poltergeist-like pull to write words, paint landscapes, film and take pictures, make music, etc., but I doubt they are as satisfying. If you're reading this, I assume you are a creative mind who feels the same. You feel a need to create and you want to indulge that feeling. I respect that. Just know I believe in you. I believe in your art—whatever it is you do. I'm not naïve enough to think that only writers, painters, musicians, photographers, and filmmakers have a monopoly on being creative. I've met software engineers and schoolteachers that are as creative in their work as any person I've met. Whatever you are striving to do, only you know if you are listening to that powerful desire inside that demands you express yourself. Regardless of what you seek to create, the fact that you are looking for inspiration to do it says a lot about you. It says that you believe you have a responsibility to fulfill your creative calling. It says that you would rather throw yourself into the fire of your passion than relax in a passive breeze of complacency.

Because you are a creative mind, this unexplainable feeling demands a lot from you. There are so many clichés of the dark and broody artist, but just as with any stereotype these generalizations have an origin rooted in reality. There's a reason why artists are some of the most volatile, emotional, moody, eccentric, out of the ordinary people you'll ever meet. It's not just because we think differently, but because we feel differently. For some reason, things strike a chord with us a little stronger. We feel certain emotions and expressions more poignantly than the average person might. Creative minds also have this natural unquenchable thirst to somehow satisfy something inside them that they can't even explain, but that always seems to be screaming to be made manifest. If you are a creative of any kind, you know exactly what I'm talking about. The persistent burden of expression that places so much pressure on our hearts and minds is as much our prison as it is our passion. It's like our insides are constantly on fire due to the things we haven't made yet. We genuinely feel that we have to create. So we do, and at any cost. We'd rather have you hate us or think we're crazy than not express everything that smolders inside of us. I believe some people were born to feel more, dream more, and need more. This book speaks to those people, to those who Steve Job's referred to as "the round pegs in the square holes." This book is for the people who believe they have a calling to create.

"I will not believe that I was put on this earth to pay bills and die."

I recently came across this quote and connected with it so much. It perfectly sums up how we should all view our daily lives. Each person's purpose may be different but regardless of what it is, it should always be, well, purposeful. I think so many people get caught up in mediocre thought, thinking that paychecks are their purpose. It is so easy to take the path of least resistance and float where the current pulls strongest. What's difficult, but infinitely nobler, is to make your passion your purpose. I completely understand that there are only a select few people in this life lucky enough to have their creative passion also pay their bills. I am fortunate enough to be one of those people and I thank God every day for it. No one is immune to the real world costs of paying rent and eating food. Even the most absent-minded artist needs a place to put his canvas and some bread to keep him going. This is even truer in our day and age when rent prices and the cost of gasoline seemingly skyrocket by the day. In many cases, the creative mind is someone who works a 9-5 job that is not necessarily related to their art. If this is you, it's so important that you ask yourself what you are doing before and after those hours spent at work, because it is in that space that your dreams will be brought to reality.

I once saw a pie chart that broke down the amount of hours in a week. Out of the 168 total hours available in a seven day span, the chart guesstimated that the average person will spend 56 hours sleeping, 40 hours working, and 35 hours performing miscellaneous but important tasks such as eating, showering, and traveling. The point of the chart was to show how many hours were left over after these demands on our time are fulfilled each week. So, out of the 168 hours the Gregorian calendar allows us each week, how much do we have left? (I have a personal policy not to engage in anything that even resembles mathematics but

maybe some of you are a little more number in-
clined than myself.)

The answer is 37 hours.

Now let us pretend that the pie chart was in-
deed gospel truth and provides an accurate repre-
sentation of your weekly life. That would mean
that each week you have a sum total of over a day
and a half to create for yourself the life you've
always dreamed of. Which leads to a second, and
much more important question: What am I doing
in the hours that don't require me to be somewhere
or to be doing something? Am I amplifying my
passions or suppressing them? Am I getting closer
to my dreams or stagnating in my current position? Think about it: if your life only consists of
time spent working and then time spent relaxing,
where in that are you actually doing what you really want to do with your life? Dreams are so much
more than slumber-induced conjurations from

our subconscious, they are a very real catalyst for achievement.

Visions of the most grandiose nature are what fuel creative accomplishment, the more unrealistic the more potent. Protect your dreams like you would defend your own life, because after all, is there really any difference? I don't think so. I believe that dreams are what make life worth living. In the immortal words of Paulo Coelho in The Alchemist: It's the possibility of having a dream come true that makes life interesting. I'm convinced I was born with those words emblazoned upon my heart. Why have average dreams? Why have a dream if you don't believe that it's the one that is going to change your life? In everything you do you should envision the best, most magical, most optimistic, and often times most unrealistic outcome happening. Why not? Considering there are actual people who have truly become overnight success stories, why can't the same happen to you? The only dreams worth having are the ones that you're sure will spectacularly change your life and the world. It's our loftiest visions and wildest ideas that make us keep pressing forward with positivity. It's always been my belief that our unrealistic ambitions are the most beautiful.

Don't just wait for dreams to come, create them. You are the only thing separating yourself from the life you've always envisioned. Don't wait around for gatekeepers to let you in, use your creativity and passion as dynamite to blow the gates apart. Creating opportunities for yourself is as important as your creativity itself. I've always said that Mr. Opportunity doesn't go knocking on doors like the popular idiom suggests. No, you have to go to his door and knock the damn thing down and then drag him to your doorstep. You'll never get what you deserve, you'll get what you hustle for. Be consistent and put constant pressure on your dreams. Sooner or later, that pressure will turn raw belief into a diamond. Believe in the incredible and magical power of a dream, and then use your ambition to force it into fruition. Another popular phrase will tell you that good things come to those who wait, but from what I've seen, good things come to those who chase after their dreams with reckless abandon.

The reason I preach creativity so fervently is because I believe one of the main purposes of this life is to create things that didn't exist before, something that will last far longer than any of us. It's about leaving this world knowing that you created things with your mind that will survive far longer than your physical body. Be remarkable. Do something memorable. I'm convinced that being average is the biggest sin I could ever commit. I want to touch the world, I want my work to stand the test of time, regardless of if it pays my bills or not. I recently came across this quote by Arthur Miller: "Don't be seduced into thinking that that which does not make a profit is without value." To me, that means that life is too short to be concerned with 401(k)'s, stocks, and politics. We aren't here to become the richest person in the graveyard, we are here to create unique manifestations that mirror our souls. What could be more worthwhile than following our mind wherever it yearns to wander? Forge a path worth traveling and then let the momentum carry you to places that truly matter. You'll never be unfulfilled chasing your dreams. Discouraged? Definitely. Depressed? Occasionally. But unfulfilled? Never. If you are seeking to make your dream a reality, then at the end of every day as you sit in consuming darkness before you relent to sleep, you will be able to look deep within and know that you remained true to every part of yourself. Selling out can be so easy and oh so tempting at times. But you must understand that even a moment of inauthenticity is a massive deviation from your creative path. By daring to vandalize the walls of conformity and blaze a trail of genuine expression, you are scorching the earth with your own unique mark. No one ever created anything important by thinking common thoughts.

Never take your ideas or inspiration for granted. The brilliance of the mind is that it can create things that are infinite. Using the creativity we possessed as children and then clinging to it into adulthood has to be among the most respectable of attributes. When we cease to create, a part of us dies. But when we capture an idea and weave it into a visible expression of who we are, we are speaking the language of souls. What is man if not a creator? What is humanity if not an opportunity for expression? This mission to keep our creativity alive is so difficult if we allow the monotony of life to creep in and contaminate the magic inside us. It is for this reason why it's so important for creative minds to surround themselves with people and places that will ignite these desires within them. I'm lucky enough to live in a city where a history of art, culture, and diversity is visible and available immediately. But I think these magical sparks of inspiration can be found anywhere; some places you just have to look a little harder. I'm also addicted to visiting new places and meeting different people. It is always so fascinating to me that even just a few hours on a plane can take us to areas where the people and culture are fundamentally unique to that location. Yet, as beautiful as this phenomenon is, diversity scares some people. Creative minds cannot afford that fear. What would life be without diversity? It should be what separates us that brings us together, celebrating and supporting one another in our extraordinary differences. The human tendency to recoil at what is foreign is one that we need to rip out of ourselves through travel, experience, education, and conversation. By embracing the diversity in others, we solidify our own individuality. I believe we should all deeply internalize Mark Twain's words when he wrote: "Travel is fatal to prejudice, bigotry, and narrow-mindedness, and many of our people need it sorely on these accounts. Broad, wholesome, charitable views of men and things cannot be acquired by vegetating in one little corner of the earth all one's lifetime."

This book will speak a lot about being in tune with what is around you. You share this earth with billions of other people so you better believe their energy can affect yours. Surround yourself with people who not only possess an inspiring ambition but who also have the selfless capacity to support others as well. I grew up in a place where a very strong and very real crab mentality existed. Just like crabs in a bucket, anytime someone sought to go above and beyond their current station in life, others would react by trying to bring them down. Upward striving was almost constantly met with downward pulling. They didn't want to see someone they knew breakthrough and go on to achieve more because of how it would make them feel about their own situation. Many people have this same attitude of 'I want to see you do well but not better than me.' Have you ever noticed how people who have never met you tend to be much more supportive than people you've been around for years? It's because people tend to feel uncomfortable and inferior by the fact that you both started in the same place but now you are progressing. Don't be like that. Believe in yourself and in those around you. The success of others won't somehow lessen yours. You're not in a competition with other people, you're in a competition with yourself to create what you're capable of creating. The only struggle you should feel is trying to successfully connect your creative vision with your work ethic. Everything else is just background noise. Don't meander in crowds that are characterized by envy and contempt. You've probably heard the common wisdom that you become the result of the people you surround yourself with most, but I think what that really means is that you absorb the energy put off by those around you. Follow your vibes, and always keep the dreams in your head pure. Set all your pursuits on fire and then surround yourself with people who carry gasoline.

While it's important to keep an eye singular to

positive influences, an entire section of this book talks solely about people who carry fire extinguishers, those who would rather criticize than create. These people are so uninvolved in their own lives that they seek to dim the light of those who shine brighter or who shine a different color than they're comfortable with. There will never be any semblance of rationale as to why some people feel the need to actively try to detract from what others are striving to do, rather than just focusing on their own situation. Don't waste your mental energy trying to figure it out. If you don't respond, they don't exist. One penny minds will never understand the attitude of a million dollar dreamer. Always remember, if you're not going against the grain, then you are being swallowed up by the current. Keep grinding, and keep shining.

One of my favorite lyrics by Kanye West says: "Now I could let the dream killers kill my self-esteem, or use my arrogance as the steam to power my dreams." I love this, and it's always been how I've lived my life. I swear if every hater/doubter/ negative person knew that they just pour gallons of mental lighter fluid on the eternal fire inside me known as my ambition, they would probably just keep their comments to themselves. Regardless of that fact, negative people will naturally always feel the need to make their uneducated opinions known. Your only response should be to keep pressing forward. The fact that they are taking time out of their day to critique something that you took the time to create puts you on a higher plane of existence right off the bat. Negative people can spit venom all they want, but at the end of the day, they're the ones who will be left screaming into darkness with no one to hear them. Any worth-while journey is going to shake the trees and make doubters come out to squawk at you. Just remember that success is the ultimate silencer, the most potent antidote for the disease of hatred. While it's an unexplainable truth that criticism always feels louder than support, it will never shine brighter. Love and positivity will always be stronger than hate and negativity.

Whatever your reason for reading this book, I hope it motivates and empowers you to continue on your creative journey, no matter the cost. I couldn't have more respect for people who choose to focus on perfecting their craft and refuse to allow anyone to tell them that making a vocation out of their art is too much of a gamble. I love to see people ignore the real world risks and just create in a genuine way. I love experiencing creativity that's been funneled straight to me, untainted by committees and capitalism. It is something that truly warms my artistic soul. I love it when a film gives me that restless burning feeling in my chest, making me want to go write. I love it when I can tell I'm listening to something that a musician poured their entire being into, something that makes me feel an emotion that yearns to express itself. In my opinion, art is the true currency. Money comes and goes, but what you create will always last. Don't worry about what is commonly done or what people say is unrealistic. Your responsibility is to your creativity, not to making other people feel comfortable. You did not have them in mind when you created these dreams inside your head. Your journey may be a winding road of detours and obstacles, but at least it will never be one of missed opportunity and regret.

The road you have chosen to travel will include the onerous task of seeking and listening to inspiration. Pay attention to your ideas and give each one the time and energy it deserves. It's funny,

I frequently come across cheesy business/entre-preneur quotes online that use macho aphorisms such as, "Ideas are cheap, execution is valuable." While I guess I can understand the intent of such a phrase, I couldn't disagree more with the view-point that ideas are common things that anyone can have. Ideas are the genesis of every great thing that has ever been created. The fact is, not every-one is capable of producing great ideas and few people give them the respect they deserve within their own mind. A true creative mind snatches any idea that floats by and then violently wrings it out to see if it has substance. Ideas are ground zero of the creative process, small flecks of gold that can become a masterful treasure. Don't dismiss the random thoughts that come into your mind. The fact that we will never know the origin of these precious imaginations is divine within itself. Re-spect your ideas by writing them down as soon as they come. Then, put them through the crucible of your creative process to see if something special comes out on the other side. You owe that to your creativity.

What lies ahead of you, dear reader, is a tangible manifestation of my mind as a passionate creative activist. This book does not exist to help you master your creativity, but rather to nurture it. I hope that this manifesto sparks your desire to create and inspires you to keep going with whatever it is you seek to do. Each individual's path is different, but I believe the messages contained here can be applied by anyone who seeks to produce something new. Lastly, I want to thank you for reading. Even though I didn't write this book for you—just like you don't create your art for others—it still means the world to me that you are reading it. I knew something magical was happening as I typed away in that dim morning light, that I was drawing out something from within that had been brewing for a very long time—possibly my entire life. Everything came together perfectly for this book to come to fruition, which further crystallizes my knowledge that I was meant to create it. If there is one thing I hope for you to learn within these next pages, it is this: creativity resides with those who remain faithful to it.

Begin Correspondence.

The following information shan't be repeated.

Commit to memory the instructions given.

I.

Little minds cannot see the nepotistic nature of the universe, while big minds do whatever is necessary to be seated favorably at the table. Never allow the dinner to begin without you, and be sure to bring a voracious appetite. As the wine pours and the steaming pots rise with vapor, eye your tablemates and carefully decide whom you can truly trust. Many different attitudes will try to take a seat for the meal, but be sure to allow only the genuine of heart. If the conversation turns to the common affairs of commoners, remind your worthy associates of the High Order to which they seek membership. Never be heard wasting minutes discussing inconsequential martyrs of mediocrity, for their unenlightened existence has no place inside a heart full of wonder. Remember, it is the pirate desires within you that make you a rose on the vine rather than a thorn. You have a calling to elevate the consciousness of those around you by transcending collective thought and acting as a ladder that delivers lost spirits from their pits of despair. This sense of duty must always be present within you, lighting your course with each bold step along the way. Never quell the ambitions that seek to make manifest your creative indulgences, and remain accountable to their yearnings inside your soul. Suffocating these internal desires is as insufferable a sin as any. Those who suppress these beautiful winds that churn inside them are spitting into it, and will only have their salivary shiftlessness spewed back at them. Always listen to the frivolous frequencies within and surrender to every one, giving each the credence it deserves. Be unabashed in your attempts to spark these vibrant hues, and remain open to their transmissions at all times, refusing to violate the divine passion that has been forged at your core. Accepting and heeding these premonitions is the key to everything you wish to accomplish. Whether transcribed in darkness or in light, your journey is yours to decide. Regardless of this choice, never miss an opportunity to spit-shine your desires in preparation for the adrenaline-filled scurry that will be set off by the awakening alarm known as inspiration. Frequently question the whereabouts of your fellow wandering dreamers who wish to join you in husking the cornfields of absolution. Reflect inward and ask if these colleagues can see the light produced by your fiery streamers of passion. Realize that keeping this luminescence burning will help to light their paths as well as your own. There is nothing more noble than inspiring others to quantify their own aura. On the other hand, sitting lazy and lachrymose over the potential dangers of your journey will help no one, and will only aid to damn you in your progression. Cancel out candid customs of complacency, and instead embrace the thought of having your torrid dreams put to the test. Clear out the firebrush fields of apathy around you in order to make way for your juggernaut engines of change, excavating the terrain of indifference and enjoying the off-road adventure upon which you are embarking. The time is always now to eschew darkness. You must make available to all the fearless elixir of self-embracing clarity, which the High Order has been

consuming for years. The tides of change have
been brewing since the beginning of man, and
it must be your belief that this tsunami of trans-
figuration can and will be the catalyst for a more
enlightened population. While many now suffer
in darkness, there is hope for the select few whose
synapses remain open to our intellectual vaccination. We are the crusaders. We are the revolution.
We are the keepers and the chasers of the future.
The all-knowing Cartographer did not have average things in mind for you when he handcrafted
your diaphragm and then breathed into you the
beginning of your journey. Believe that you have
been built differently, constructed to dwell on a
higher terrace than the masses, born to fearlessly
seize the fortuitous opportunities that are made
available to nearly everyone, but are only seized
by a rare collective that can move in a direction
of tangible action. Develop a plan by which you

will base these mobilizations, carefully marking, dotting, scribbling, and doodling everything that your heart desires. By permanently placing these conjurations onto the highest shelf inside your mind, you will be showing the universe that you value the weight and wonder of your aspirations. You will see that your dreams become much more attainable after you graciously acknowledge their presence and allow them to swell inside you like an early morning typhoon. Keep in mind that these dreams may change as you circumvent convention throughout your journey. You may one day reach up to that highest shelf within and find that the texture and feel of these divine embodiments have changed shape. While some dreams form early and remain solidified throughout the entirety of a person's expedition, some dreams come later, while others end up being unforeseeably altered into different visions altogether. None of these truths are less important than another. Regardless of how they begin, you must always listen to your dreams as if you were fine-tuning an old transistor radio, seeking to find the most crisp, clear station to speak beautiful orations to your mind. This is that broadcast. This is the rebellion. Internalize the impending declamation, and take solace in the knowledge that it is a noble quest to be a disrupter of the accepted.

II.

Blitzkrieg the cowardly corporations with your open awareness of their misdeeds. You must make them understand that you are no longer a marionette that is subject to the inconsiderate movements of their wretched wrists. Become a variable, an unquantifiable figure that can't be marginalized into taking any one particular shape. Express complete indifference toward instructions that instruct the masses to become slaves to their instructors. Your inner rebellion will be the outward insignia upon which both light-seekers and dark-dwellers will identify you, drawing the light-seekers to join and respect you, while causing the dark-dwellers to demonize your existence. Do not launch your insurrection for the purpose of earning a superficial patch of rebellion, but do so because you are honoring your creative indignation that deserves to be acted upon. Do not disrupt for the sake of disruption, but because it is in your nature to do so. This attitude of genuine individuality will further spark truth inside you, and will also serve to heat the chests of your fellow comrades. Join together as a band of like-minded believers who storm the battlefield of bureaucracy with strikes of well-calculated mayhem. The key is to take advantage of and become the chaos. Exploit the arbitrary restrictions to which these wicked organizations are bound and use them to breach the outer walls. Their power lies in the great stone fortresses they have built around their workings, but their infrastructure remains weak. To successfully penetrate these walls, it is necessary that you sacrifice your insecure associations with any beings who have helped to build them. These ignorant individuals will not understand your vision and will only seek to drag you down as you move forward. Transcend the menial custom of wasting time in maintaining superficial relationships. If another being does not inspire you, motivate you, create with you, elevate you, or simply generate positivity within and around you, you have a responsibility to your journey to cut them loose. Meaningless connections can quickly dim even the brightest of lights. Unwrap their succubus cords from around you and allow them to become chaff in the wind. Obtain the proper weaponry—by subterfuge if need be—and then strike with thunderous anarchy. Throw dynamite into caves of doubt and hang nooses from the gallows of creative infidelity. You must illuminate every inch of the dark crevices that seek to reduce the saturation in the world around you. Broadcast these dusty corners to the outside world so the people can see what truly goes on behind their aching backs. Become an arsonist of adventure. Become a minister of malcontent. Never be intimidated by the immensity of the journey ahead of you; your potential will always loom much larger. Take pleasure in the enormity of your mission and bask in the glow of your every success, while still maintaining an insatiable appetite for more. Give encouragement to your fellow crusaders who have the strength to press on, while stepping over those who fall to the pressure of marble floors and golden décor. Passionately adjudicate the actions of those around you by cutting loose the drifters and solidifying your bond with the true players. Remind them that the reward of this journey will be one that does not materialize into a tangible embodiment of wealth. As you explore the intricate corridors of your mind, always place the greatest importance in owning a freedom that cannot be put on a leash and yanked backward from chasing the tires of free expression. Undoubtedly, you will hear the regal bells of skyscrapers ding-donging in vicious reprimand of your beautiful quest, but you will ignore these annoying attempts to dissuade you. Internalize the contempt of the suit-and-tie clusters that look upon your pursuit with confused callousness, using their salty tears and sanctimonious screams as gasoline to fuel your journey. All of these omens are leaves in the tea that will prove you are moving in the proper direction. Press on toward the forest of conformity, and begin cutting with a ludicrous zeal, using the wood to light a raging fire that will consume everything you have exposed. Let the heat eradicate the smell of oppression and replace it with ash, savagely painting the stratospheric canvas with an all-consuming cloud of smoke. Propagate the death of the propaganda that has been forced down the esophagi of the uninspired. When their structures have crumbled and the dust sits dormant in the air as if time has stood still, bathe in the righteousness of your quest. While ambition has been and always will be the oil in your eternal engine, do not forget to carve out a moment of present awareness to celebrate the road behind you, while still keeping your eyes on the road ahead. If this ability to remain in the now is forgotten, the most satisfying moments in life can be cheapened by your futuristic vision. While it is no simple task for members of the creative breed, you must enjoy current celebrations while still focusing on what is to come. The past holds much warmth, the present holds much beauty, and the future holds much wonder. The successful amalgamation of these three truths is the key to a happy life. Embracing each one while honoring their distinct importance is an ongoing exercise in emotion that you will practice throughout your voyage.

The common man's sickening philosophies will always linger in the air around you like a foul stench, seeking to discourage you from continuing your mission. Heed them not. The common sense rules of their uninspired world are simply a fragile collection of socially reinforced illusions. While the resistance of buildings and leaders may quickly fall to your insurrection, their poisonous teachings can remain stuck to concrete minds for centuries. Be particularly leery of the massive structures that promise learning, but in actuality only dole out ample servings of carefully contemplated conformity. See through the thick glass of moneychangers who grab greasy dollar bills and silently cackle as their fortresses grow in power and wealth. Never subscribe to their poisonous proposition that you can only be what they teach you to be; their debauched documentations will have no bearing on the success of your enlightened quest. Shun their blaring white walls and concrete carpeting, and choose to breathe the mist of uninhibited freedom instead. You will depart from this overly trodden path that the vast majority of dark-dwellers travel, all the while sifting through the debris of their spiritual destitution. Cautiously observe this unenlightened empire in order to chart your course around its well-placed obstacles. Ask yourself where these highly trafficked roads lead, and then turn one hundred and eighty degrees to violently crusade in the opposite direction. Paint your ship with the blood of doubt and remember that success is not the title of the destination, but the motivator of your expedition. Understand that the ideal of concretely defined achievement is something that the masses have established. You will not become a checker of their checklists. You exist to fly beyond these pre-determined endpoints. Spread your wings and know that there is no such practice as flying too close to the sun; the warning of that long-held myth is not applicable to your altitude of ambition. For if you have the necessary strength and ingenuity to successfully reach the sun with makeshift wings, there is no doubt that you are capable of sprouting natural wings when they are most needed. Leave the perception of what is impossible to the imposters. You will always find comfort in your quest to master the indeterminable quality of creativity, a quality that will inspire you as quickly as it can evade you. You must never try to harness it. Let it breathe within you as the gas inside your lungs fills and empties now. Allow it to consume you whenever it so mysteriously calls upon your mind, and invite it to stay as long as it will oblige. Caress it, feed it, and worship it. Cancel your subscription to any false prophet that claims it can be bottled up and digested at any time. The moment you buy into the belief that there is a formula for producing it at will, you will be jettisoned backward in your progression. Remember that creativity is an emotion, not an attribute. It is not a synthetic service that can be called upon, but a phantom persuasion that calls upon you. Embrace the fact that this magic cannot be saddled, but rather must be ridden bareback and held onto tightly as it whisks you away to unforeseeable horizons. The moment you remember to forget what they have taught you will be the moment you become exactly what you need to be. The monotony of everyday life is the primary carcinogen that drives wild hearts mad. A propensity for creation is what has liberated those before you, will liberate you now, and will be the source of liberation for all who come after you. Your only obligation is to honor this desire and allow it to be. It will flow steadily, while never fully taking shape, like a colored swirl of smoke. Observe as it ebbs and flows inside your being, manifesting its mercurial nature to come and go as it pleases. Make room for it by clearing out any sycophantic desires within yourself. This emotion can feel any disingenuous motives and if it does, it will escape you in a reprimanding flash of lightning. Much of your life's journey will be spent learning what your creativity wants and needs in order to dwell inside you. Seek inspiration as if you were seeking oxygen. Search for unknown places rich with color, diversity, and personality. Consume pure forms of media that will expand your mind, and reject the refuse that blares loudly into the dull ears of the commoners. Seek raw rewards of real life experience, and recognize that the state of illumination is often only achieved in the darkest of corridors. Be prepared for the times during which you must poison your mind in order to draw out inspired creations from the depths. You must also be vigilant in paying attention to the manifestations born from the minds of others. This will serve to broaden your vision and motivate you to continue crafting your own unique voice. Construct a comfortable homestead inside your mind where you can drink steadily from the warmth of your creative glow.

IV.

Throughout the course of your creative journey, you will come across individuals who will stand against your cause and seek to oppress you. Without exception, these beings will have placed a surety in their inadequacies of behemoth proportions, causing them to battle and belittle your every move. Unseen by the naked eye, these imposters carry an immovable weight upon their shoulders that will inevitably transform them into snarling beasts of envy. While you seek to create art, the only thing these purposeless people will create is animosity. Some may even masquerade as your fellow confidants for a season, but as time passes they will become coarse toward your constant striving and commit small treasonous acts that will eventually lead to an open dissent of you and your journey. When they are not actively seeking to douse your passion with their fire hoses of negativity, these frail minds will proselytize to your doorsteps with toxically wrapped defilements that symbolize their lack of ambition. Never indulge them. Shoo them away without a moment's hesitation. While making your way through this filthy demographic, the purity of your mission will force these small harlots to come face to face with their true selves, reminding them that their time in the sun will never arrive so long as they continue to operate in a darkness of their own construction.

Make them aware that the paper they seek to carry
in their pockets will not equate to an ascent to the
pedestal upon which they have placed their idols.
Be careful and act swiftly as you operate among
their spiteful hostility; their infection can quickly
turn you into a diseased member of their epidemic
of complacency and whoredom. These nasty
symptoms of free-flowing hatred and negativity
are ones that can so easily taint your own mind.
Revolt against this faction's pathetic pornography
and shatter their closed doors into splinters, expos-
ing their pastime of staying on porches of criticism
and enjoying lounge chairs of scorn. Their path
is much easier than the one you have chosen to
pursue, but do not be tempted by its hollow pleasure. Common minds critique, while great minds
create. As they carry out their egregious exercises
in a risk-free environment, you will continue to
risk everything, knowing that only fools fall into

the lackluster trap of mocking those who believe in the power of their beautifully unrealistic ambitions. The inescapable truth is that the majority of these ordinary beings will live out and finish their lives in an uninspiring flicker of self-doubt and unhappiness. There will always be this group of vitriolic bottom-dwellers who seek to infect the High Order and those striving to be a part of it. You must come to terms with the fact that their cancer is incurable and will never be eradicated among this population, the next one, or any to come. Some of these individuals may appeal to the humanity inside you by relying on the social bonds that time and circumstance have created between you, but you will not waste energy trying to drag along these parasitic carcasses; yours is a path upon which they will never belong. The only proper vaccination against these vermin is your constant vigilance. Reach into your keen mind and create an unbreakable barricade of confidence, positivity, and ambition. While you only have power over the fulfillment of your own journey, this does not mean it is the only one worthy of your attention. Always be observant of what your fellow creative-minded travelers are producing in their own inspired missions. By taking inventory and evaluating the authenticity of their creations, you will quickly be able to distinguish who is bound for the glory road, and who is wearing a cloak of disguise. Those who only pretend to be makers will slowly tick down like bitter alarm clocks, and will eventually end up screaming at the true creators with envious vomit. Serenade the loyal constituents with your positivity and seek to collaborate with them, taking inspiration from what they've developed during their own travels. See this shared journey as a cordial competition. Both members and seekers of the High Order are always able to identify those cut from their same cloth. Respect this sacred society that you belong to by magnifying the calling that it demands from you. The commoners have a phrase that they vilify called 'blind ambition.' This term, while sneered at by the uninspired, is one of the most common attributes shared by those who comprise the High Order. Know that there is nothing negative about having this one-track mind, this singular focus of conjuring up dreams and forcibly shaping them into reality without permission from the outside. Freely indulge your ambitions and careen into the unknown with a reckless abandon. The result of your constant forward-throttle will be the surpassing of limits that make others return to the comfort of their small homes. As you speed down this highway toward fulfillment, the fumes from your engine will light the night sky with an aurora borealis of hope. Let all eyes gaze at the magic you create. Paint these vibrant teal and fuchsia hues by unapologetically streaking into the atmosphere, paying no attention to the uninspired patrolmen who seek to blare their disparaging sirens at you as you rumble the ground they stand upon. There will be many exits, detours, re-routes, rest stops, and pit stops, but you will not touch your brakes until you see the skyline of satisfaction on the horizon. Your safe arrival to this glorious destination will depend largely on your ability to decipher the maps that the all-knowing Cartographer has designed with you in mind. Pay careful attention to how the universe unfolds in front of you, and then respond with a series of enlightened counter-moves, all the while taunting the naysayers with the beauty of your inspired vision.

V.

Imperative to the success of your journey will be the understanding and overcoming of the one enemy that could upend your entire course. This nefarious nemesis is known by many names, but is most commonly referred to as Fear. The crippling unpleasantness that this monster can evoke from within is something that has created countless martyrs amongst humanity. Only a choice demographic has the strength to overpower the pain, discomfort, humiliation, and failure that this sinister black tar creates and uses to rapidly entrench its victims into immovable statues. Look around you and see the everyday beings that have allowed this soulless creature to stop their progression. Observe the lives of those who have made a home for Fear inside their hearts, and ask if their outcome is one that you wish to replicate. If you are a true seeker of the High Order, your answer is already known. While the evasion of this plague is paramount, it is important to understand that even the greatest of creative crusaders are, and have always been, susceptible to it. It is simply inhuman to be completely unfazed by this dark feeling's natural tendency to cloud the mind. But those upon the ivory mountaintop who you seek to join have done either of two things to dismiss Fear, one of which you must choose as your own solution. First, if your level of confidence is strong enough, it can be utilized as a weapon to tranquilize and bury this furtive feeling deep beneath the self-assured soil of your soul. There it will rattle the ground occasionally, but will remain power-less so long as you never uncover it. Let it sink into the solid ground of your conviction, weaken-ing further and further in the permafrost of your persistence. Nothing will erode this protective barrier if you continue to nourish the topsoil that is your inner belief. The second option is much less confrontational, but takes a centeredness that few can muster. This option requires that you carefully allow Fear into your home, but then hypnotize it into a docile motivator that dwells dormant in the basement, chained and harnessed to the floor-boards. It is here that you will occasionally allow Fear—in small doses—to be the effective motiva-tor that it can be. Only the wise understand that feeling Fear's radioactive glow can be a positive catalyst for creation. Note how those of the High

Order have used the Fear of mediocrity to propel themselves out of ordinary circumstances. Just remember: it is critical that you only employ this method in small ingestions, not massive digestions. Never feed this ghoul with any crumbs of doubt, jealousy, or insecurity; if it receives even a taste of these unsavory attributes it will rapidly multiply in size and gusto. Keep moving forward and you will have no problem leaving this negativity in your wondrous wake. In the end, the method you choose when dealing with Fear will not be as important as your simple resolve to renounce its power. Never let it distort or taint your lucid vision in any way. Remaining diligent in your quest for glory will leave no time for serious consideration of such noxious notions. Your ambition must act as a foghorn that cuts through cloudy hazes of uncertainty like a blade through water. Whenever darkness falls like thunder and threatens to destroy the castle you have built with your unique magic, you must be adequately equipped to call forth the greatness within you to dispel it. Liquid fire may rain down from the heavens and lick the very soil upon which you stand, but you will never bow to Fear's evil expectations. Bring rose-colored enchantments with you wherever you go to eliminate quarrelsome negativity that can indeterminably delay your journey as quickly as it began. There is no power on this planet or on others that has the ability to forcibly hijack your will. It is only if you allow dark discretions to drip into the ocean of your belief that you will see a cancerous contamination of the pure waters within you. The best method of filtration is to be omniscient when it comes to these wailing whispers. Respect the culmination of all the varied emotions you feel and silently meditate as they dance within you. The good and bad vibrations sent to you from the universe will be unmistakable markers that point you toward your desired destination. It is only when you combine these lessons from your life experience with unmitigated searches for inspiration that you will find yourself in a position capable of pure anarchic alchemy.

VI.

Always keep in mind that the assault you are waging on the world will be one fueled by dreams, but not the sort that take place during a state of slumber. The most powerful dreams are the type formulated while awake—the kind that put pressure on the chest and make the stomach tight. Impetuously embrace these grand visions that make the heart race and your body feel wearily electric. Allow your ambition to hold you hostage from any sort of rest or relaxation. While the others sleep, you will dream. As they drink their bottles of toxic levity, you will be a pink glowing comet cascading confidently through the night sky. While the others laugh with riotous thunder at their cynical gatherings, you will be submarining through the depths among the squids and the whales. While the weak-minded drop to the dirt with intellectual exhaustion, you will be whizzing through the landscape until the end of the tour. The uninspired will never know what it is like to lose sleep over incessant thoughts that gallop inside the mind. Let your motivation keep you awake with a furrowed brow, propelling you into a forward-thinking frenzy. *When, where*, and *how* are all afterthought technicalities; *must, can*, and *will* are the manifestations of true resolve. Sit up in the darkness plotting your path to prosperity, and as the world around you continues to percolate in a grey mass of densely populated perception, you will surge through the

smog in a fervent pursuit of something different. This desire to bring into existence something
unique, something that the world has not yet seen,
is the definition of purity. Never stray from this
holiest of missions, which is to create something
that survives far longer than your tabernacle of
flesh and bone. For when your outer shell de-
scends to rejoin the dust from which it was spawn,
these manifestations of your mind will continue
breathing and intertwining into the beautiful helix
of the universe. Embody this mission for creation
by being a symbol of free thought and individuality. Never allow anything or anyone to repress your
urges to create; true creators would rather die than
be unable to express these natural impulses. To not
be allowed free expression delivers an unbearable
and torturous death to the imaginative soul. The
High Order is comprised of these rare spirits that
know no bounds in their petition for inspiration.

The world cannot afford to have them operate in any way other than that which their personal constitution demands. Too many lives are spent idly drifting downstream, bouncing off of dull rocks and eventually becoming entangled in the moss of mediocrity. Never allow this self-satisfaction to stain the translucency of your creativity. The measure of your life will not be weighed on some grand and golden scale, but rather by a divine discernment of your intangible contributions. The size of your creations—be they small, medium, or large—will have no bearing in this judgment. Instead, the criterion of this far-reaching decision will be based upon the unadulterated passion that you exhibit throughout your life and the number of those who draw inspiration from it. For there is no greater act than awakening in another being the desire to create. These precious provocations continue the series of invaluable chain reactions that have taken place since the beginning of time. This formula of seeking inspiration, and in turn inspiring others, is the eternal paragon of creation. Continue to build upward on this bedrock until your steeples reach the stars, all the while keeping your doors open to allow the warm winds of originality to blow through. Fill the pews of your daily life with unique characters that are rich with experience and diversity. Keep a constant appetite to live fully, inspire widely, love deeply, and create unsparingly. Remember that the recipe for a satisfying creative existence will never include the pursuit of excess. If destiny allows, wealth and notability may become a validating byproduct of your creations, but they should never be your sole intent. The chasing of such vain and terrestrial tantalizations will only burden you with unnecessary weights of worldliness. The true makers bleed their masterpieces from veins of pure expression, not hollow materialism. Become free from the vapid expectations surrounding you and forge your own story, making the figments of your imagination come to life like brilliant shooting stars firing into a cobalt sky. Be unceasing in your hunt for illumination, while never allowing circumstance to lessen your pace. Wherever you stand, wherever your traveling feet take you, continue to create with passion and your expedition will never lose the vibrant light needed to guide it. Share your journey with like-minded cohorts and enjoy creations from their perspective as you move along in similar focus. Stay away from the tarnished heads that wish to impel your inner belief and decrypt your safeguarded heart. Seek to create magic inside of every moment so that your well of imagination always runs full, ready to be drawn from at all times. Don't forget that nobody remembers tomorrow, and the kisses of the past only stain the lips of those burdened by the disease of nostalgia. Create present fulfillment while still thoughtfully yearning for future opportunity. Fill your glass with the rejuvenating liquid of moments, for the most elaborate lives are built on their tapestry of existential enjoyment. We can haphazardly carry briefcases from ever-fleeting yesteryear and tie anchors of the past around our delicate necks, but the existence of the hour we now inhabit can never be resurrected. The overlaying truth of the old world has remained the same for the new: passion ushers progress.

End correspondence.

Afterword

One of the main themes highlighted in what you've just read is that we should always honor the universal truth that inspiration to create comes from consuming what others have created. There is profound wisdom in the quote commonly attributed to Pablo Picasso that says, "great artists steal," as well as the biblical wisdom that "there is nothing new under the sun." We are all being inspired by what others have created, and then hopefully, in turn, are inspiring others with our own creations. For this reason, it is my artistic obligation in this afterword to not only give thanks to those closest to me, but to give proper salute to the people and places that have inspired me the most. The sources of inspiration listed below have, in some way or another, directly influenced me to create the book that you now hold in your hands.

My Sarah – I could fill notebooks with my love and appreciation for you (and I have), so I will keep this brief by saying that you are in my heart with every step I take and in my mind with every word I write. No accomplishment could ever come close to the knowledge that I get to spend the rest of eternity with the love of my life.

Mom and Dad – You've always raised your kids to believe that anything is possible. I cannot recall a single time during my childhood when I did not feel completely validated and supported in even my most grandiose notions. Thank you for all you've sacrificed for me and for always supporting my dreams.

Tiffany, Ryan, and Chantel - Tiffany, thanks for always being the strong first-born sibling and showing us all what Superwoman aspires to be like. Ryan, I've spent my entire life idolizing my older brother and nothing has changed; you have been and always will be one of my heroes. Chantel, you and I seem to share the same creative gene in the family, and it has always been a welcome respite to talk to you about artistic endeavors. I always brim with pride when showing people your work.

Everyone else – Kyson Dana for letting me enjoy (i.e. use and abuse) your artistic talents time and time again. This book would still be just a Word document if it weren't for your help. You'll always be my go-to guy for things like this, whether you like it or not. Brittany Tennant for contributing your hawk eye to the editing process. Your contributions and input were invaluable; your grandma will be proud. Tim McConnehey for believing in a first-time author and having this book's best interest in mind from the beginning. My deepest thanks go to you and Izzard Ink for helping my creation to see the light of the day. Trent Kennedy for always being the number one fan of my writing; you'll always see manuscripts first. Elijah Silva for being my artistic soul brother. KC Barnes for your constant and unwavering support in everything I do. Clay Olsen for your creative heart and for creating something that has allowed me to live the life I've always pictured for myself. Salinas, California for being the setting of my life story's transformation. The Salt Lake Film Society for being my sacred sanctuary of inspiration.

My High Order – Allen Ginsberg for helping me to find my true voice as a writer. The first time I read your work, I felt a very real unlocking inside my mind that has motivated me to become the writer I was always meant to be. Paulo Coelho for changing the way I see my journey in life; *The Alchemist* will forever be one of the most divine, inspired works ever created by man. Peter B. Kyne for the endless motivation I've received from *The Go-Getter*; I'll never stop chasing the blue vase. J.K. Rowling for creating a truly magical world that will always be a fond part of my life and will continue to inspire millions. Steve Jobs for inspiring me with your incredible passion and elevated vision. Kanye West for always doing it your way and inspiring me with your angst over creation. Macklemore & Ryan Lewis for being unflinching examples of independent artists. James Franco for your inspiring passion in fearlessly creating. Claude Debussy, Erik Satie, Dave Brubeck, Maxence Cyrin, and Pandora's Yoga Radio Station for being the soundtrack to my wordsmithery. Charles Duhigg for sending encouragement and validation to an aspiring young writer; it meant more than you know. Filmmakers/writers Noah Baumbach, Alex Ross Perry, Sam Esmail, and Wes Anderson for inspiring me with your incredible voices and unique visions.

And last but not least, I want to thank all the people I have and will come across in my life who are defined in Section IV of this book. Your scorn, doubt, and negativity have always been just as valuable as any of the above positive sources. Thank you for the fuel.

- Robbie Tripp

About the Author

Robbie Tripp is a wordsmith, public speaker, and creative activist. He is the author of Create Rebellion, and is also a contributing writer to *The Huffington Post* and *The Californian*. He is particularly proud of the following accomplishments: visiting 49 of the 50 United States in one summer to raise awareness for organ and tissue donation; founding the Salinas Writer's Circle at the John Steinbeck Public Library in Salinas, California; meeting with former U.S. President Bill Clinton in the Oval Office of the White House; and scoring on 15-time NBA All-Star Shaquille O'Neal in a 1-on-1 basketball game.

Outside of writing, Robbie enjoys watching independent film, listening to jazz, running, playing basketball, and eating sushi.

He currently lives in San Francisco with his beautiful wife, Sarah.

For more, visit www.robbietripp.com

Notes

CPSIA information can be obtained at www.ICGtesting.com
Printed in the USA
BVOW06s0231130816

458772BV00017B/190/P